Fixing Performance Problems: A Leader's Guide

Common Sense Ideas that Work

OTHER BOOKS BY
BUD BILANICH

Supervisory Leadership and the New Factory

Using Values to Turn Vision into Reality

Four Secrets of High Performance Organizations

Leading With Values

Praise For Bud Bilanich's Previous Books

Using Values to Turn Vision Into Reality

"A simple but powerful book. Read it!"

Ken Blanchard

"Refreshing and useful. Effectively takes important leadership concepts and brings them to life."

Peggy Williams, President, Ithaca College

"An excellent 'how to' book on turning vision and values into value-added results."

Eric Harvey, Co-author "Walk the Talk…and Get the Results You Want"

4 Secrets of High Performing Organizations

"Elegantly simple."

Karen Katen, President, Pfizer Global Pharmaceuticals
Executive Vice President, Pfizer Inc

"Simple but powerful concepts."

Chase Carey, CEO, Fox Television

Praise For Bud Bilanich's Previous Books

"Full of wisdom that applies to leaders of all types of organizations."

> John Arigoni, President and CEO,
> Boys and Girls Clubs of Metro Denver

"Any leader, from CEO to mail room supervisor, will find easy-to-use ideas in this book."

> Ron Guziak, Executive Director, Hoag Hospital Foundation

Supervisory Leadership and the New Factory

"This book is must reading for anyone interested in managing an effective manufacturing organization."

> Tony Maddaluna, Vice President Manufacturing, Europe
> Pfizer Inc

Advance Praise for "Fixing Performance Problems"

"This is a book I wish I had when I was beginning my career as an HR generalist."

Sylvia Montero, Senior Vice President Human Resources,
Pfizer Inc

"A practical, no nonsense approach to solving common, and often undiscussed, work problems. An easy to use guide that managers and supervisors can use to help them with one of the most important parts of their jobs."

Mila Baker, Vice President Learning and Leadership Development,
Dana Corporation

"Dr. Bilanich has once again provided his readers with an easy to read, practical guide for managing performance. His new book provides simple, common sense ideas on fixing performance problems. This information is particularly useful in manufacturing environments. It provides an excellent guideline for middle managers and supervisors to use when dealing with difficult performance issues."

J. R. Mulkey, Director of Operations,
Adams and Brookhaven Plants, Minerals Technologies, Inc

Advance Praise for "Fixing Performance Problems"

"As entrepreneurs, we know first hand the importance of fixing performance problems. Bud Bilanich's book is full of common sense advice on this subject. Anyone who owns a small business should read and study it."

Jack Davis, Rob Likoff, Founders, Group DCA

"In *Fixing Performance Problems*, Bud Bilanich provides invaluable common sense ideas for anyone who manages people. He also effectively demonstrates how blogs can be used to develop book content. The comments Bud received from real world leaders who read his blog posts on performance problems helped him make this an even more useful book."

Denise Wakeman and Patsi Krakoff, Psy.D.
The Blog Squad

As Always . . .
To Cathy, my muse

Acknowledgements

Writing a book is not easy. However, this one was made easier because much of the content started out as posts to my blog: www.CommonSenseGuy.com. Therefore, I'd like to thank Patsi Krakoff and Denise Wakeman of the Blog Squad who set up my blog and helped me get going. I also would like to thank the people at TypePad for putting together such wonderfully intuitive software that makes my blog posting easy and fun.

Eric Harvey provided some good advice about moving the project from a series of blog posts to a book. Bobbi Benson did a great job designing the book and its cover. Janet Gelernter's editing and proofreading assistance was invaluable.

Cathy, my wife, partner and friend was patient with me as I wrote. She dealt with both of me — Bud Jekyll and Bud Hyde — with unconditional love.

Finally, I'd like to thank the people who read my blog. Their comments and e-mails convinced me that I was on to something with my posts on performance problems. Without them, this book never would have been published.

Bud Bilanich
Denver, CO

Fixing Performance Problems: A Leader's Guide

Common Sense Ideas that Work

Bud Bilanich

A Front Row Press / BookSurge
Joint Publication

ISBN: 1-4196-1746-X
Library of Congress Control Number: 2005909856

Available through Amazon.com and at bookstores everywhere.

Large quantity orders are available from BookSurge, LLC:
    www.booksurge.com
    1.866.308.6235
    orders@booksurge.com

Table of Contents

Table of Contents

"Executives owe it to the organization and to their fellow workers not to tolerate bad performing individuals in important jobs."

Peter Drucker

"All jobs are important."

Bud Bilanich

Introduction

"The endurance of any organization depends on the quality of its leadership."

Chester Barnard

In over 30 years as a management consultant, executive coach, keynote speaker, workshop leader and author, I have had one type of request for service more than any other: fixing performance problems. While I have assisted many leaders in fixing performance problems, I prefer to teach my clients how to do it themselves, and not rely on me. There is nothing more fundamental to a leader's job than getting the best out of the people he or she leads.

Over the years, I've learned that performance problems vary from individual to individual, and situation to situation. Just as no two performance problems are exactly similar, there is no silver bullet — no one best way of fixing them. On the other hand, I have found that most performance problems fall into one of eleven categories, and that leaders can use a similar approach to fix problems that fall into a specific category.

In this book, I describe each of the eleven categories, give you an example from my personal experience, and then suggest what to do to fix performance problems that fall into the category.

When you finish reading, you should have a good idea of how to identify the eleven most common types of performance problems and how to fix them.

However, as I always tell my audiences, "knowing is not enough." If you're going to succeed as a leader, you have to put these skills to use. Sometimes, it's not pleasant. But, if you're going to lead, you have to deal with and fix performance problems. This book will tell you what to do. It's up to you to actually do it. Good luck.

Bud Bilanich
Denver, CO
November, 2005

Chapter One

⌒✌⌒

Leadership and Performance

"It is not the critic who counts; not the man who points out how the
strong man stumbled, or where the doer of deeds could have done better.
The credit belongs to the man who is actually in the arena; whose face is
marred by dust and sweat and blood; who strives valiantly; who errs
and comes short again and again; who knows the great enthusiasms, the
great devotions, and spends himself in a worthy cause; who at the best
knows in the end the triumph of high achievement; and who at the worst,
if he fails, at least fails while daring greatly; so that his place shall never
be with those cold and timid souls who know neither victory nor defeat."

Theodore Roosevelt

Okay. You're a leader. You're in the arena every day. You have
people reporting to you. You count on them to get the job

done, because your performance depends on their performance. No matter what your title – Manager, Supervisor, Team Leader, Director, Vice President; or your job function – Customer Service, Sales, R&D, IT, Manufacturing, Distribution, Tech Service, Marketing; or your industry – Manufacturing, Distribution, Financial Services, Retail, Transportation; your most important job is to ensure that your people do their jobs well.

No man will make a great leader who wants to do it all

himself, or to get all the credit for doing it.

Andrew Carnegie

Most people do a good job most of the time; a few of them cause occasional problems; all of them probably screw up every once in a while. That's why you have a job. Face it. You're a leader. You have to deal with performance problems: it's your job. You're in the arena. You might say: "I don't have the time, I have too many other things to do — budgets, reports, dealing with customers, etc." Nothing could be further from the truth. You're a leader, you have to get things done through your people. You can't do it all yourself. You have to make time to fix performance problems.

There's no one fix to all performance problems. Every performance problem is unique to the individual and situation. However, there are some common reasons for performance problems. Here are eleven of the most common.

1. *People don't know what they are supposed to do.*

2. *People don't know why they should do what they are supposed to do.*

3. *People don't know how to do what they are supposed to do.*

4. *People think the prescribed methods will not or do not work, or think that their way is better.*

5. *People think that other things are more important.*

6. *People think that they are performing in an acceptable manner.*

7. *Non-performance is rewarded*

8. *Good performance feels like punishment.*

9. *There are no positive consequences for good performance.*

10. *There are no negative consequences for poor performance.*

11. *People encounter obstacles they cannot control.*

Identifying the problem is not enough: you have to fix it. In the pages that follow, you'll find a detailed look at each type of problem, and some common sense ideas for fixing them.

Chapter Two

Problem #1

People don't know what they are supposed to do.

"We struggle with the complexities and avoid the simplicities."

Norman Vincent Peale

Norman Vincent Peale's advice applies here. At first glance, this may not seem like a reason for poor performance at all — many leaders say: "Of course people know what to do, they don't need me to tell them." Wrong! You need to go to great lengths to ensure that your people know exactly what is expected of them. If you're not specific about your expectations, you can't blame your people if they don't meet them. You can blame only yourself.

Setting expectations and making sure that people know what they are supposed to do doesn't need to take a lot of time. In his famous book, *The One Minute Manager,* Ken Blanchard calls it "One Minute Goal Setting." In all fairness, it takes more than a minute — but not much.

Several years ago, I was working with a sales manager. He was very frustrated by one of his better salespeople. While the rep was meeting his quotas, the manager thought that he could exceed them by putting in a little more effort. The manager expected that his reps would make at least 25 calls per week, an average of five a day.

This particular rep had some loyal and solid customers. He was meeting his quota, but only making about three calls a day, an average of 15 per week. The manager was frustrated because he thought that the rep could be closing more sales if he made more calls.

Most of what we call management consists of making it difficult for people to get their jobs done.

Peter Drucker

When I asked the manager if he had ever told this rep, and the other reps who worked for him, about his 25 calls per week expectation, he said: "No, they know that I expect them to be out there making calls, that's enough." Obviously it wasn't, or he wouldn't have been having problems with this rep.

As it turned out the rep really didn't know the manager's expectations. He assumed that as long as he was meeting his sales quota, it didn't matter how many calls he made. His focus was on results. The manager's focus was on increased activity — which he was confident would lead to improved results. This was a classic case of the sales rep not knowing what he was supposed to do.

To fix this type of problem, you need to make sure that your people know three things:

1. *What needs to be accomplished;*
2. *The deadline for accomplishing it;*
3. *What successful completion of the goal or task looks like.*

The sales manager had expectations regarding the number of calls his reps would make in a week. He should have been, and has since begun, conveying this information to his sales people in a few simple sentences. For example:

"Joe, I expect that you will see at least 25 customers per week. This works out to an average of five per day." (1. *What needs to be accomplished.)*

"I want to receive your weekly call reports for all 25 of the calls by Friday at 5:00." (2. *The deadline for accomplishing it.)*

"I want the call reports e-mailed to me. You should use the standard call report form. Make sure you complete the form accurately and completely — especially when you're updating the customer contact information. Don't forget to provide at least one or two sentences of narrative about the call. It's not enough to just check the boxes. I want to see what's going on with the customer, so I need you to complete the narrative part of the form too." (*3. What successful completion of the task looks like.*)

Armed with this information, Joe can plan his week. He'll need to budget time for making calls, and for reporting on those calls. He will realize that making 25 calls per week and reporting on them is as important as meeting his quota. Without this information, Joe assumed that meeting quota was his one and only performance indicator. He now knows that making the prescribed number of calls is just as important — and that making more calls is likely to result in more sales.

The common sense leadership point here is: *If you don't tell people exactly what you expect of them, they will decide for themselves. You're better off telling them, than letting them guess.*

Chapter Three

~~~

Problem #2

People don't know why they should do what they are supposed to do.

"Leaders don't force people to follow — they invite them on a journey."
Charles S. Lauer

If people are going to join you on your journey, they need to understand why you're asking them to do things your way. There are two reasons why people should do what they are asked to do and in the manner they are asked to do it: 1) it is the right thing to do for the business; and 2) it is the right thing to do for the individual.

As I explained above, you first have to make sure that your people know: 1) what they need to accomplish; 2) the deadline for accomplishing it; and 3) what good performance looks like.

But this is not enough. You also need to take the time to explain why these three things are important. Tell your people the reasons behind your expectations. Make sure your people know:

1. *The business reasons and benefits of the performance standards for which they are accountable.*

2. *The personal benefits that will accrue from performing in the expected manner.*

A few months later, the sales manager I described in the previous chapter called me. He was having another performance problem with Joe. As you recall, the sales manager told Joe that in addition to making his sales quota, he wanted him to make 25 calls a week; to e-mail his call reports for the week to him by Friday at 5:00; to complete the form accurately; and to include narrative comments for each call. He did a good job of clearly stating his expectations of Joe when it comes to calls and call reporting. Joe now knows what he is supposed to do. The manager thought the problem was fixed.

Leadership and learning are indispensable to each other.

John F. Kennedy

However, while Joe kept making his quota and hitting or exceeding the 25 call per week standard, he began to be late on his call reporting, and submitting reports with incomplete information. It seems that Joe was merely checking off the boxes on the form, and not completing the narrative for most of his calls.

This was a different type of performance problem. Joe knew what to do — he just wasn't doing it. In this case, the probable cause was Joe not knowing why he was supposed to do what he was supposed to do. The sales manager tried calling and e-mailing Joe and explaining the standards again. This didn't work. Joe knew the standards.

We decided that the manager needed to speak with Joe and explain how complete (narrative included) and on time call reporting benefits both the business and Joe. I coached him to say something like: "Joe, I need you to complete the narrative section on every one of your call reports for two reasons:

1) I need to have a clear picture of what's happening with all of the accounts of all of the people I manage. I can't be with you on every call, so I rely on your notes to keep me up to date." *(The business reason for the performance standard.)*

2) "These notes will benefit you too. They're not important at the time you write them, but you'll find that they'll really come in handy when you're planning your next call with this customer." *(The personal benefit to the employee for meeting the standard.)*

Once they had this discussion, Joe understood both the business reason for completing his call reports on time and thoroughly, as well as the potential personal benefits that come from doing what he is supposed to do. After this conversation, he got his act together and began submitting his reports complete and on time.

The common sense leadership point here is: *Some people will resist doing what they are supposed to do, because they don't see a good reason for it. Leaders need to be clear on: 1) the business reasons why something needs to be done; and 2) the benefits to the individual for doing it and doing it well.*

Chapter Four

∽⌒

Problem #3

People don't know how to do what they are supposed to do.

"Teachers open the door, but you must enter by yourself."

"Tell me and I'll forget,
show me and I may remember,
involve me and I'll understand."

"Give a man a fish and you feed him for a day.
Teach a man to fish and you feed him for a lifetime."
Chinese Proverbs

This reason might surprise you at first. After all, don't the people who do the job know the most about it? No, not if you don't teach and train them first! You need to open the door so your people can walk through it and perform well.

Don't make assumptions about what your people know and don't know about performing their job at a high level. Training, and retraining, is often what it takes to fix this type of performance problem.

A good leader inspires others with confidence in him; a great leader inspires them with confidence in themselves.

Anonymous

Teaching someone how to perform a job is not that difficult. In fact, it can be broken down into a simple, five-step process, based on the Chinese proverb of "tell, show, involve."

1. *Tell the person what to do.*

2. *Show the person what to do.*

3. *Observe the person as he or she performs the task.*

4. *Reinforce correct or effective performance.*

5. *Redirect incorrect or ineffective performance.*

Follow these steps and the people you lead will have the

knowledge and skills necessary to perform in an effective manner. Here's an example: internal audit groups have faced a lot of heat since the passage of the Sarbannes Oxley act. Audit leaders have had to train or retrain their people. I came across an excellent new auditor training program at one of my clients. It illustrates the proper implementation of the five-step training process quite well.

1. *Tell the person what to do.* Prior to sending a new auditor on an audit, audit managers conduct one-to-one discussions with the individual. They review the company's audit plan, and the steps to conducting an effective audit. They describe the process in detail and answer any questions that the new auditor may have.

2. *Show the person what to do.* New auditors' participation in their first audit is limited to observation. They observe their manager and a colleague conducting an actual audit with a real client. They are told to observe closely, make notes and to ask any questions they might have about the audit process at an end-of-the-day meeting. Audit managers focus on setting a good example, by conducting the audit in the prescribed manner. They provide a positive role model by demonstrating the appropriate manner for conducting an audit.

3. *Observe the person as he or she performs the task.* Audit managers always accompany new auditors on their first

audit. They allow the new auditor to take the lead. They intervene rarely — only in cases where the audit has gone seriously off track. They stay in the background and observe the auditor as he or she goes about the task of conducting the audit. They share their observations at the end of the day.

4. *Reinforce correct or effective performance.* Audit managers begin the end-of-the-day wrap-up sessions with a discussion of what they observed the auditor doing correctly in the audit. They are specific in their comments. Their goal is to ensure that the auditor understands what he or she did well, why it is important, and that they should continue to behave in the same way. If audit managers have done a good job in steps one and two, they have a lot of positive feedback to provide auditors in this step.

5. *Redirect incorrect or ineffective performance.* In these end-of-the-day wrap-up meetings, audit managers also provide auditors with specific examples of areas in which their performance can be improved. They describe specific situations they observed in the audit, what the auditor did, why it is problematic, and what the auditor should do differently in the future.

The example above describes an auditor training process. However, it can be applied to sales training, manufacturing operator training, customer service training, supervisor training — almost every case in which a person needs to learn exactly how to perform a job. If you apply it effectively, you'll stop a lot of potential performance problems before they start.

The common sense leadership point here is: *Make sure your people know how to do what you expect them to do. If they don't, teach them.*

Chapter Five

Problem #4

*People think the prescribed methods
will not or do not work, or believe
that their way is better.*

*"Leading is the art of dealing with humanity,
working diligently on behalf of the people you lead,
being sympathetic with them, but also insisting
that they face their problems squarely."*
S. L. A. Marshall

Recently, I was in a shopping mall. I saw a young mother with three kids; two were in a stroller and another was walking alongside her. She was wearing a T-shirt that read: "Because I'm the Mommy, that's why." I got a chuckle out of the shirt. But then I began to reflect on how many managers and leaders use the "because I'm the Mommy" style of leadership.

Today's well-educated employees don't buy this leadership style. They are less likely to accept it. As "The Who" say in their rock opera, *Tommy:* "We're not going to take it." Today's employees will challenge instructions that don't make sense to them. They will make their position, questions and concerns known. As a leader, you can't say: "I'm the boss, that's why." You have to deal with their questions and concerns in an open and respectful manner. You must be sympathetic to their thoughts and concerns while insisting that they fix their performance problems.

Several years ago, I was working with a VP of Manufacturing for a generic drug manufacturer. When I arrived at his office one day he was visibly upset. I asked why. He told me that he had just been on the phone with an FDA auditor. The auditor told him that one of his products was repeatedly failing the quality test that was on file with the agency. He said: "So I called my Quality Director and asked him about it. He said, 'don't worry, we've switched to a better, more scientifically sound test.'" The VP was frustrated because his Quality Department did not inform the agency of this change in testing procedures. So now they were not in compliance.

This was a serious issue. The FDA has the power to shut down a pharmaceutical manufacturing facility that is not in compliance with its regulations. It also was a serious performance problem, and one that is directly related to this reason. The Quality Director believed he had a better way of testing. However, what he didn't understand was that it was not enough to develop a better testing protocol. He needed to get approval for it by the FDA and amend the documents on file with the agency. He thought this was a waste of time and effort. In this case, he didn't understand the ramifications of his actions.

It is impossible for a man to learn what he

thinks he already knows.

Epictetus

To fix problems like these, you need to apply a three-step, common sense approach.

1. *Make sure the other person understands what is expected of him or her.*

2. *Make sure the other person accepts what is expected of him or her.*

3. *Make sure the other person can do what is expected of him or her.*

Understanding is about the head. If you want people to do something in a prescribed manner, take the time to explain not only how to do it, but why it is important to do it that way. For example, many manufacturing organizations, especially with time sensitive raw materials, work on a "FIFO" (first in, first out) basis. In other words, raw materials should be used in the order in which they were received. This means that raw materials should be rotated as they are delivered by material handlers. Raw materials delivered last week should be placed in front of raw materials delivered this week. This ensures that fresh raw materials are always available to the operator.

However, fork-truck operators might find it easier to drop new raw materials in front of the ones that are already there. In regulated industries like pharmaceuticals and food processing, this is a violation of the policies and procedures established by the government. In non-regulated industries, this practice can result in using out of date materials, or having to discard otherwise useable, but obsolete, materials. In either case, this drives up manufacturing costs.

If you're a leader in this type of situation, you need to make sure that your people understand the potential negative consequences of not following FIFO procedures. Explain not only the procedures, but the logic behind them. In many cases, this is enough to address the performance problem.

Acceptance is about the heart. Understanding is a good start. But it's not always enough. To continue with the example from above, material handlers may understand the reasons for FIFO procedures and what they are supposed to do in order to comply with them. But complying with FIFO procedures makes the material handler's life a little more difficult. He or she has to rotate the raw materials every time a delivery is made. This takes more time, and could be seen as a waste of effort — regardless of the potential regulatory or financial costs associated with not performing in the prescribed manner.

In this situation, you won't get very far by explaining the reasons for, and logic behind, the FIFO procedure. Instead, you'll have to engage the other person in conversation. Listen to their reasons for continuing to not follow procedures. Empathize with them — it's okay to admit that rotating raw material stock is more time consuming. Often, the mere act of listening to, and empathizing with, an individual's concerns is enough to get the person to change his or her behavior.

If this doesn't work, try another tack. Ask the employee to suggest an alternative method. If you do this, make sure you set clear boundaries. In this case, the real issue isn't rotating the raw materials, it's ensuring that the raw materials received the earliest are used first in the production process. If the employee comes up with a method that ensures compliance with the FIFO policy, and is easier for him or her, make the procedural changes necessary to accommodate the new and better way of doing things. People like this, as it shows that their thoughts and suggestions are welcome and acted upon. This always leads to acceptance. Even if employees cannot come up with a better alternative, they tend to be more accepting of the procedures in place, as they realize that they had an opportunity to change them, but could not devise a better way. Just being invited to participate goes a long way to ensuring acceptance.

People ask the difference between a leader and a boss. . . .

The leader works in the open, and the boss in covert. The

leader leads, and the boss drives.

Theodore Roosevelt

Doing is about the hands. It also is the leadership intervention most often used inappropriately. If an individual does not understand or accept instructions, merely showing him or her how to do things the right way is not going to help. It's like speaking louder in English to a non-English speaking person. All it does is frustrate both parties.

If a person does not understand the reasons why he is being asked to do something, or doesn't accept those reasons, training or retraining him or her is not likely to solve the problem. In fact, training may make the situation worse.

Here's a real-life, and somewhat embarrassing, example. When I was a young guy, I wasn't great at managing my money. I had a bad habit of not completing my business travel expense reports on time. Why? Because I had spent my travel advance, but didn't have legitimate business expenses to cover the amount of the advance. In other words, I owed the company money, and I needed to wait until pay day to square up.

After about six months of late expense reports, my boss asked me to come into his office. He sat down with an expense report and showed me how to complete it properly. He tried to show me how to do something — complete the form. He was treating the situation as if it were a "hands" problem. Only my problem was a "head," not "hands," thing.

I was embarrassed to admit that I was doing a poor job of managing money. If he had asked for reasons why I wasn't getting my expense reports in on time, I might have told him of my money management problem. He might have been able to give me the value of his experience in managing travel advances (as I've done a few times in my career when I managed young people who were just starting to travel for business). Who knows what might have happened. All I know is that by attempting to solve my expense report performance problem by focusing on "do," my boss made the situation worse, not better.

On the other hand, there are times when focusing on "do" is the correct thing to do. For example, a sales manager may notice that a salesperson is doing a poor job of integrating sales aids into his or her sales presentations. This may be because he or she: a) doesn't get the importance and usefulness of sales aids (*understand*); b) doesn't like the sales aids provided, and would rather use his or her own (*accept*); or c) doesn't know how to use sales aids effectively (*do*).

If the answer is "c", he or she doesn't know how to use sales aids effectively; some remedial training is the way to go. If it is "a" or "b", training on how to use sales aids is not likely to be effective.

The common sense leadership point here is: *Identify the reason behind why an individual is not performing. If it is a "head" issue, explain the reasons behind what he or she needs to do. If it is a "heart" issue, listen to, and empathize with the person, and see if he or she can come up with an alternative that meets all of the requirements of the job. If it is a "hands" issue, show them how to do things the right way.*

Chapter Six

$\sim$

Problem #5

*People think that other things
are more important.*

"*Leadership is lifting a person's vision to higher sights,
raising a person's performance to a higher standard,
building a personality beyond its normal limitations.*"
Peter Drucker

Several years ago, I was consulting with a wood-working
manufacturer. This particular company manufactured stair
parts. Turned balusters were one of their big products. A turned
baluster is a vertical support on a stair: it is usually shaped by a
lathe. You've seen them many times.

This particular plant was having some serious quality problems.
After spending some time on the floor, I was able to pinpoint the

problem. Blanks were loaded on to a lathe that turned twenty of them at one time. The equipment was old. As a result, it tended to vibrate quite a bit. After a while, these vibrations caused the lathe to create out-of-spec balusters. Usually, these balusters were turned off-center, and were unusable. It wasn't even possible to rework them. They were simply scrap — a waste of operator time, raw materials and utilities.

I asked the lathe operator if he had any ideas why this was happening. He said, "yeah, these machines are old. We set them up at the beginning of every shift and after lunch, but they vibrate out of spec before we set them up again."

Leadership is practiced not so much in words

as in attitude and in actions.

Harold Geneen

When I asked him why he didn't stop the machines and recalibrate them when he saw they were beginning to vibrate out of spec, he said, "I can't do that. I have to produce so many of these a day. If I stop to reset the lathe, I won't make my production quota."

"But you're producing scrap," I said.

"That's not my problem. I worry about production, not quality," he replied.

This is a perfect example of people thinking that other tasks and activities are more important than doing the entire job right. A good friend and client, Nat Ricciardi, calls this phenomenon the *"tyranny of the or."* Good leaders take people's performance to a higher standard and help them surpass their normal limitations by not settling for the *tyranny of the or.*

In effect, the lathe operator was really saying: "What do you want, production or quality?" Sales managers complain about sales people who say: "What do you want me to do, call on customers or fill out call reports?" The answer to these questions, of course is: "Both. I want productivity and quality. I want sales calls and completed call reports."

This is what Nat would call *"the genius of the and."* The lathe operator's supervisor needed to make it clear that he expects him to meet production targets *and* meet quality standards *and* do it safely *and* do all this in a manner that complies with all the regulations that govern manufacturing.

To fix this type of problem, you need to employ the *genius of the and.* Make it clear to the people who work for you that most jobs are multi-faceted. They have multiple priorities that are equally or almost equally important.

Don't let your people be governed by the *tyranny of the or.* Instead, use the *genius of the and* to ensure that all priorities are addressed.

So the common sense leadership point here is: *Make sure the people who work for you know and understand all of the priorities that guide their work. Don't let them be governed by the "tyranny of the or." Instead, have them use the "genius of the and" to guide their behavior.*

Chapter Seven

Problem #6

*People think they are performing
in an acceptable manner.*

*"If I accept you as you are, I will make you worse;
however if I treat you as though you are what you are
capable of becoming, I help you become that."*

Johann Wolfgang Von Goethe

I could just as easily have called this problem — "people are not receiving honest feedback on their performance." Several years ago, I came across an article lampooning astrological signs. I am a Leo, born August 14. The Leo symbol is a lion: bold, self-assured, king of the jungle. In the humor article, the writer described Leos as follows: "You think you are a born leader, other people think you're pushy." I got quite a chuckle out of that one. I do think of myself as a leader. And, quite frequently, people have told me to back off and let someone else take the lead.

The humorous astrological description applies here. We all see ourselves in the best light. In the absence of feedback to the contrary, most people will assume that they are doing okay. Telling someone that he or she is not doing a good job is not an easy or pleasant task, but it's the only way of helping people see what they are capable of becoming. Effective leaders give this gift to their people. People who do not receive feedback are unlikely to change their behavior.

Facts do not cease to exist because they are ignored.

Aldous Huxley

There's an old joke about a guy who goes to a coffee shop every morning for breakfast. The waitress is terrible, she gets the order wrong, doesn't refill his coffee unless he asks for it, spills coffee on the table when she does get around to it — you get the picture. One day, he's there with a friend who comments on the poor service. The first guy sighs and says: "Yeah, it's this way everyday. I keep giving her big tips, but she never seems to get better."

She's never going to get better, because she's getting big tips — positive feedback. She probably assumes that she's doing a pretty good job. After all, she is getting good tips. If she got no tip, she might take a look at her service and make some changes in how she does her job.

The employment laws were written with this idea in mind. If people are not made aware of the fact that their performance is not up to standard, it is unfair to discipline or dismiss them. You need to explicitly tell your people when their performance is poor. You also need to provide them with an opportunity to turn around the problem before taking disciplinary action. If you don't, you're in trouble. Courts have ruled over and over again that employees were dismissed without just cause.

People will assume that they are performing in an acceptable manner unless they are told otherwise. Effective leaders provide their people with regular feedback. In this way, good performers know they are doing a good job and poor performers know where they are not up to standard and what they need to do to get there.

Here's a sad story that illustrates this point. About ten years ago, I was working with a company that was in the process of reorganizing its manufacturing operations. They had been organized along functional lines — manufacturing, packaging, quality control, equipment set-up and maintenance, etc. They decided to go to a product-based structure in which small groups of people were responsible for all of the work associated with a specific product line. This was a fairly big shift in the way work would be done. Job descriptions were rewritten. Everybody in the plant was going to be reassigned to newly created jobs and work units.

In order to spread out the talent in an equitable manner, they decided to hold a "draft," much like the NFL or NBA. Only in this draft, the personnel would not be athletes coming out of college, but employees currently employed on site. As it turned out, the new structure required one less person than the old.

When the draft was completed, there was one individual, "Bob," who was not drafted. He was a 20+ year employee, who had worked in almost every department in the plant. His reputation among his coworkers was poor. People joked about him — they would take bets on how long he would last every time his job changed and he was reassigned to another department. He was viewed as a problem employee — by everyone but himself. Managers at the plant where he worked periodically shifted him from one department to another. When he was reassigned to a new department, the receiving manager would joke that it was his or her turn "in the barrel for the next couple of years."

Prior to announcing the new structure and department assignments, the HR manager spoke to Bob and explained to him that he had not been drafted, but that since he was a long service employee, the company would find something for him to do. Bob was incredulous. "What do you mean I wasn't drafted? I'm one of the most valuable people around here. Nobody has worked in as many different departments as me. I know this place better than anyone," he said.

Lead and inspire people. Don't try to manage and manipulate people. Inventories can be managed but people must be led.

Ross Perot

Bob had a point. Every time he was transferred, his boss took him aside and said something like: "Bob, you're doing a great job here, but they have a problem in this other department. We need you to go over there and help us out. I hate to lose you, but this is for the best of the company."

Bob believed his bosses. Who wouldn't? After all, wouldn't you rather see yourself as a "born leader" than "pushy"? Bob did. He never got any negative feedback in twenty years. It was logical for him to assume that he was doing a good job, maybe even a great job, as he was "needed" in so many different departments.

Bob's bosses did him a disservice. If somewhere along the line, someone had told him that he wasn't cutting it, he might have been able to improve his performance. Instead, he spent twenty years living a lie, never knowing that his performance was poor.

The story has a happy ending. Once Bob wasn't drafted, he realized that he needed to change. He dove into his new job and did it well. He never became a stellar performer, but he never again was the butt of jokes told behind his back.

The common sense leadership point here is: *Provide everyone who works for you with honest feedback on how well they're doing. People shouldn't have to guess. In the absence of feedback to the contrary, people will assume that they are doing well. It is naïve to think that they will improve their performance or change their behavior. They'll be guided by the old maxim "if it ain't broke, don't fix it." Feedback, especially negative feedback, is one of the toughest parts of a leader's job, but it is one of the most critically important.*

Chapter Eight

Problem #7

Non-performance is rewarded.

"Few things help an individual more than giving him responsibility,
and letting him know that you trust him."
Booker T. Washington

When I was a kid, there was a joke that went like this. "When I was growing up, we were so poor that all I had for lunch was a wish sandwich."

"What's a wish sandwich?"

"It's two pieces of bread and you wish you had some meat or cheese."

That brings us to reason number seven for poor performance — *non-performance is rewarded.* The guy who kept over-tipping a bad waitress was eating a wish sandwich. He kept wishing that she would get better, but in actuality, he did things that encouraged her to keep on screwing up.

There are many ways to reward poor performance. Here are four of the most common:

1. *Fix the problems that your people make.*

2. *Take away the difficult or unpleasant jobs that your people do poorly.*

3. *Promote or transfer problem people to get them out of your organization.*

4. *Give too much attention to problem performers.*

In his famous Harvard Business Review article, *Management Time, Who's Got the Monkey*, William Oncken tells this story. A manager is sitting in his office. It's late Friday afternoon in the summer. He has a lot of things planned for the weekend, including a lot of "honey do's" he promised his wife. At 3:00, one of the people who works for him comes in and says, "we have a problem," and lays out what, in fact, is a problem that needs to be fixed soon. The manager says, "Okay, let me work on it over the weekend, and I'll get back to you on Monday." At 3:30 another one of his people comes in with a different problem. The manager's response is the same.

This happens again at 4:00 and 4:30. As he's driving home, the manager is frustrated. His plans for the weekend are now on hold, because he's going to spend Saturday at the office working on the problems his people brought to him late Friday. As he's driving to the office Saturday morning, he has to go by the local golf course. As he drives by, he looks over and sees his four subordinates out for a round of golf. This is a prime example of reason number 1: fixing the problems that your people make.

Sometimes it seems easier to fix a problem yourself than to have the person responsible fix it. William Oncken refers to this as *subordinate imposed time*. He characterizes it this way: subordinate imposed time begins the moment a monkey (something for which the subordinate is responsible) successfully executes a leap from the back of a subordinate to the back of his or her superior. It does not end until the monkey is returned to its proper owner for care and feeding. By accepting the monkey, the manager has made himself subordinate to his subordinate. He goes on to say that even if a manager takes on only a couple of monkeys a day, by end of the week he may have ten or more. He spends his time doing his subordinates' work. In Oncken's terminology, leaders who fall victim to problem number one — fixing problems that their people make — are accepting their peoples' monkeys. They need to give them back.

The common sense leadership point here is: *Don't clean up your people's messes. Make them do it. Guide them, give them suggestions and help, but make them solve their own problems.* You're really giving them dual gifts: responsibility and your trust.

Tony Maddaluna, a friend and client, has a sign on his desk that says *"dbmapwoas."* It means *"don't bring me a problem without a solution"* — good monkey management advice.

Let's take a look at the second way to reward poor performance. There's an old cynical saying: "Work your fingers to the bone, and what do you get? Bony fingers." This saying applies here. The fix is simple: don't take away the difficult or unpleasant jobs that your people do poorly.

The employer generally gets the employees he deserves.

Walter Gilbey

When people continually screw up a certain job or jobs, many leaders give up, and take away those jobs. They give them to someone they can trust. Pretty soon, the one or two people who they can trust are doing all the work, while everyone else is coasting. They have a couple of people with bony fingers and a bunch of others who are fat, dumb and happy.

You need to make sure that you don't reward poor performance. Make sure everyone carries his or her own weight. Insist that all of your people do a good job on the jobs for which they are responsible. Coach, advise and teach, but hold people accountable. Just as you don't want to take on your people's monkeys, don't let your people pass their monkeys to their colleagues. The common sense point here is: *Hold people responsible for doing their jobs. Keep the workload fair and evenly balanced.*

Problem three is even worse than problem two — and it happens more often than you might think. Several years ago, I worked with a company where there was a running joke: "How do you get a cushy job at headquarters?" The answer: "Screw up really badly. We never fire anybody, so you'll get out of here and get an easy make-work job there." This is bad.

Good management consists in showing average people

how to do the work of superior people.

John D. Rockefeller

Never reward poor performers with promotions and transfers. Instead, do your best to turn around poor performance. Failing this, work on an exit strategy. The common sense point here is: *Don't pass your problems on to someone else in the organization by promoting or transferring poor performers. Fix the problem, don't pass it around like a box of Cracker Jack.*

The last problem is easy to slip into. Most leaders are problem solvers. They like to fix problems, so they spend most of their time with problem performers. Spending a disproportionate amount of time with problem performers raises two potential problems: 1) problem performers are getting a lot of attention — something they might not get if they performed well; and 2) good performers are not getting recognized for their performance.

Some people are starved for attention. They prefer negative attention to no attention at all. They are like children who throw tantrums when they feel their parents are not paying enough attention to them. It's easy to fall into the trap of meeting people's attention needs by spending too much time with problem performers. *Don't give problem performers undue attention. Let them know that you are not happy with their performance, give them some ideas on how to fix their problem, but make them fix it themselves.*

If you do this, you'll free up time to reward good performers. People continue to do the things for which they get rewarded. Recognizing good performance is a much better use of your time than constantly looking over the shoulder of your poor performers.

The common sense leadership point here is: *Don't reward poor performers with too much attention. Instead, recognize and reward your good performers.*

Chapter Nine

~~

Problem #8

Good performance feels like punishment.

"I admire the Good Samaritan for picking up people on the side of the road, but I don't want to be the Good Samaritan. I want to fix the road to Jericho, so people don't get beat up there."
Martin Luther King, Jr.

Let's go back to the old saying "Work your fingers to the bone, and what do you get? Bony fingers." Bony fingers are a symptom of good performance being punishing. Good performers often find themselves picking up people on the side of the road — by being asked by their leaders to clean up other people's messes.

I know that you don't set out to punish good performers, but I bet that you often do. You probably reward good performance by giving more work to your good performers — often in an attempt to take up the slack for those people who aren't carrying their weight. It's a natural reaction. When someone does everything you ask of him or her, and does it well, he or she becomes the logical choice to clean up messes or take on new and challenging projects.

When I was a young guy, I was a caddy. I liked being a caddy. I was outside, I got good exercise, and I met nice people. One of these nice people even sponsored me for the caddy scholarship that helped pay my way through college. A lot of the members at the country club where I worked liked me: many of them would request me. In general, this was a good thing.

But it could be a bad thing too. Mrs. Simmons was a case in point. Mrs. Simmons was about 80 years old. In her day, she had been a very good golfer. However, as she got older, her skills and strength diminished, while her passion for the game did not. She played nine holes every day at 8:00 am. She usually shot about 70 for those nine holes. On this course, 70 was par for 18 holes. Mrs. Simmons hit the ball pretty straight. The problem was she hit it way too often — and she took forever between shots.

A round with Mrs. Simmons went something like this. Give her the driver, watch her hit the ball 50 yards, put the driver back in the bag, walk the fifty yards, give her the three wood, watch her hit the ball another 50 yards. Repeat this cycle — giving her different clubs as she got closer to the green — several times.

Once she was on the green, Mrs. Simmons studied every putt as if it were her opportunity to win the US Open. Once she sunk the putt, the process began again by giving her the driver. This went on for nine holes and three hours.

Mrs. Simmons could be very critical of caddies. But, for some reason, she liked me. She would often request me. More often than not, Eric, the caddy master, would accede to her wishes, and I would spend a morning trudging along beside an old lady, stopping every fifty yards. To top it off, Mrs. Simmons wasn't even a very good tipper. In short, I was being punished for being a good performer.

I learned that a great leader is a man who has the ability to get other people to do what they don't want to do and like it.

Harry S. Truman

Eric would make it up to me. If I would caddy for Mrs. Simmons in the morning, he would assign me some of the better golfers (and tippers) in the afternoon. This was good, but small consolation as I trudged along with Mrs. Simmons.

I have a coaching client who regularly gets punished for her good performance. She came to me originally to ask for help in managing relationships with her peers. As we talked, it became clear that the main reason for her problems with her peers is that her boss is punishing her because he can count on her.

This woman is the General Manager of a large division of a very large company. She is very bright and a hard worker. She has an amazing capacity for multi-tasking. She can work on any number of things at one time and do them all well. Her boss, the president of a multi-billion dollar business, has come to rely on her to fix problems. For example, when something comes up in Asia (not her area) he says "we're having this problem in China, find out what's really going on, and tell me what you think we should do to fix it."

When faced with such a challenge, she immediately swings into action. She works the phones and e-mail, asking hard questions and demanding answers. She gets the people who work for her into the act too. They spend long hours sifting through the information until they have a good handle on what's happening (often she ends up knowing more about the business in China than the General Manager of China). Then, she decides on a course of action and spells it out for her boss.

Her boss then calls the Chinese GM and tells him what he wants him to do to solve the problem. Through all of this, my client and her lieutenants work late, sometimes missing family obligations. Usually after the crisis has passed, she finds that other things that require her attention have been put on hold while she was dealing with it, resulting in more long days. In effect, she gets punished by having to work long days because she can be counted on to understand and solve problems.

What's even worse, however, is the punishment she gets from her colleagues. As a group, General Managers are a pretty territorial lot. They don't like it when someone from headquarters starts asking questions of their people. They like it even less when they get detailed directions from headquarters on how to fix their problems and/or run their business. They can't take it out on the President, so they turn their wrath on my client. She gets punished by her peers because they resent what they see as her intruding on their turf.

Truth be told, she is part of the problem. She likes the challenges she is given, so she accepts them regularly. However, she has created extremely high expectations on the part of her boss. These expectations force her to work long hours and earn her the enmity of her peers.

With my help she is slowly working her way out of this hole, but it is a long process. Our biggest problem is convincing her boss that, by relying on her to solve other people's problems, he is in effect punishing her. It's slow going, but we're getting there.

After all, her boss has a good thing going. He gets his problems solved, and he doesn't have to risk the wrath of his people by holding them accountable for fixing their own problems.

This is a pretty extreme example. However, it is easy to slip into this type of inadvertent punishment. The common sense leadership point here is: *Don't punish your good performers by overworking them. Hold everyone responsible for the performance of the part of the business for which they are accountable.*

On the other hand, the system may be the culprit when it comes to punishment. One of my clients is experiencing this problem right now. He has promoted a capable, but very young person into a position of significant responsibility. Good for him, he has recognized talent and has moved to develop it. However, he is having problems adequately compensating this individual. His company has a fairly rigid compensation system. It's typical of most big company systems — pay ranges with steps in each range.

In this case, the young person promoted has moved up approximately five pay ranges. He should have received about a 50% pay increase just to bring him up to the minimum of the pay range assigned to the job into which he has been promoted. However, the company has a policy that says no one can get more than a 20% pay increase — even when a promotion is involved. This is usually not an issue, as most people do not get as large an increase in responsibility as this individual.

In this case though, it is an issue — because of the system. At some point, the manager runs the risk of seeing a decrease in the performance of this person because of the inequities of the pay system. The common sense leadership point here is: *Don't use the excuse "it's the system" to punish your good performers.*

Leadership is understanding people and involving them to help you do a job. That takes all of the good characteristics, like integrity, dedication of purpose, selflessness, knowledge, skill, implacability, as well as determination not to accept failure.

Admiral Arleigh A. Burke

One last example. I travel frequently. When I rent a car, I usually rent from Avis. I am an Avis "Preferred Member." You can be too, just sign up on-line. The main advantage to being a preferred member is that you don't have to wait at the counter to get your contract. You go directly to the bus, and get taken to your car — which is usually running with the trunk open. It is a good service for the frequent traveler.

Recently, I rented a car at an airport. I got on the bus, but when we got to the lot, the driver took me to the counter, not my car. I had to wait in line behind five or six other people, all of whom were frustrated. Not being very patient by nature, and being used to a very different service level, I was frustrated too. There was one person working the counter.

When I got to the front of the line, the agent was very apologetic for the wait. Because of his customer-friendly attitude, I didn't let my frustration show. Instead, I chose an empathy tack. I said something like: "You're really busy today. What's going on? Usually, the cars are ready."

The employee looked at me and said: "Yeah, I know. It's always like this on Monday afternoon. We have a lot of weekend rentals at this station. People bring them back on Monday, and we have to wash and gas them. We always get backed up. I've tried telling my boss that we need more people to work on Monday because of the volume, but he won't put on any more people."

You'll never see a better example of punishing someone who does a good job. This agent was a good guy. He really cared. He wanted to do a good job for his customers. He even had identified the problem. However, his leader punished him by ignoring his suggestions. Don't do this to your people.

The common sense leadership point here is: *Listen to your people when they suggest ways to handle problems. Don't make their work more difficult by ignoring their suggestions.*

Strange as it may seem, it's easy to fall into the trap of punishing good performance. If you're a leader, pay attention. Make sure you avoid these pitfalls.

Chapter Ten

Problem # 9

*There are obstacles to performing that
the individual cannot control.*

"Leaders don't inflict pain. They bear it."

Max DePree

A s I've mentioned, your most important job as a leader is
helping the people you lead to succeed. This sometimes
involves smoothing the way, or as Max DePree says, bearing the
pain. Why? Because obstacles outside people's control do exist,
and are more common than many leaders would like to admit. It's
your job to identify these roadblocks and to eliminate or minimize
them whenever possible, or to show people how to deal with
those that can't be removed.

When people tell you that they are facing serious obstacles to their performance — things beyond their control and not of their own doing — you have to get involved. You have to take the point and show them the way.

In their excellent book, *Walk the Talk*, Eric Harvey and Al Lucia share some interesting examples of company-created obstacles to performance:

> *A sign identified the location of Bill's next learning experience: The Museum of Corporate Contradictions. Bill found a two foot square glass case. Inside the case was a small pedestal that supported a single paper clip. "Where's the display? There's nothing here but a paper clip." "That's it!" replied Clarence. "The paper clip is the display. Do you know how many people have to approve buying one carton of those clips, and how long it takes to get them? Two. Two people have to approve them, and it takes two weeks to get them. If it's two approvals and two weeks for paper clips, you can imagine what it must be for other things."*
>
> *The next display item to capture Bill's attention was a red metal case labeled 'Supervisor's Tool Box.' Bill unsnapped the latch and lifted the lid. "It's empty!" he exclaimed. "There's nothing in here." "Seems like that could be a big problem," acknowledged Clarence. "If you want to get the job done, you've got to have the right tools. Either you've got them when they hire you, or the company's got to give them to you. But I've seen a lot of supervisors walking around here with empty tool boxes.*

They're doing the best they can, but they could do a lot better."
These examples really make the point about obstacles. As a leader you need to make it easier for people to do their jobs. Just as no one should have to wait two weeks for paper clips, no one should be asked to do a job for which they don't have the skills. Also, no one should have to jump through a lot of bureaucratic hoops in order to do their job.

Everything we shut our eyes to, everything we

run away from, everything we deny, denigrate or

despise, serves to defeat us in the end.

Henry Miller

Here's an example from personal experience of having to jump through bureaucratic hoops. There is a credit card issuing bank that shall remain nameless here. It espouses excellent customer service as a value. It has gone to great lengths in its marketing materials to proclaim that "Customer Service is Our Number 1 Priority." Employees are urged to "focus on the customer" and "do whatever it takes to create satisfied, loyal customers." However, some employees have found that the bank's practices make it impossible for them to provide good customer service. One of these people is the spouse of a friend of mine. She told me the following story:

> *Occasionally, a customer's payment is not credited to his account. In this case, the customer is asked to provide a copy of the canceled check as proof of payment. Most customers are okay with this. However, once they have done so they expect the bank to credit their account.*

> *The bank, however, has a policy stating that no credit can be made to an account without a corresponding debit to the account to which the funds have been erroneously applied. Customers are told that their account will not be credited until the bank determines the location of the misapplied funds.*

> *This is good accounting practice — for every credit, there must be a corresponding debit. However, it is a terrible customer service practice. In effect, the bank tells customers "we screwed up, and we admit it, but we will not fix your problem until we get our act together internally." As you can imagine, customers don't like this.*

Customer service reps are caught in the middle here. They are attempting to provide excellent customer service, but find themselves hamstrung by bank policy. The policy in question makes perfect sense from a financial control perspective, but none at all from a customer service perspective.

In this case, it's up to the bank's leaders to remove this obstacle to effective customer service. They must come up with a new practice that will allow the bank to maintain effective financial control without compromising customer service. They created the problem, and they, not the employees, need to fix it.

Processes don't do work, people do.

John Seely Brown

In my experience, there are three types of situations that create obstacles to effective performance.

Situation 1: Policies, procedures and practices exist that prevent people from performing at a high level. The bank situation I described above is typical of this one. The common sense action here is pretty simple. Review your company's policies, procedures and practices. Identify and change those that make it difficult for people to perform well.

One company I know created a *"Stupid Policy Alert Form."*

Everyone was invited to identify policies, procedures and practices that got in the way of doing their job effectively. They were surprised by how many responses they got, and how easy it was to eliminate or change the policy, procedure or practice.

Charles Dugan, a senior executive with Commerce Bank, a large consumer bank in New Jersey and New York, tells me that one of their operating principles is "no stupid bank rules." That's a great start in eliminating obstacles to effective performance.

Situation 2: People do not realize that they have the wherewithal to remove or overcome an obstacle. The common sense solution here is pretty simple too. Reinforce and publicly recognize people who take risks to point out and change problem practices. Reward people for identifying and fixing obstacles. Don't make them go crazy just trying to get someone's attention.

Situation 3: People do not have the skills necessary to do what it takes to perform well. Make sure that you clarify your expectations and that people have the skills necessary to do what it takes to perform well. Set them up to succeed, not fail.

Two factors come into play here: employees' *willingness* and *ability. Willingness* is all about commitment and confidence. Your people need both in order to be able to perform well. The example you set, and the guidance you provide, will go a long way toward building your people's commitment and confidence. *Ability*, on the other hand is about skills. And skills need to be developed and nurtured. The best way to do that is through a combination of coaching, formal classes, on the job training and specific, ongoing feedback.

So the common sense leadership points here are:

- *Make it easy for your people to do their jobs.*
- *Identify and change policies, procedures and practices that are obstacles to good performance.*
- *Listen to your people when they point out something that needs to be changed so they can do their job better.*
- *Make sure people have the skills and tools to do a good job.*

Chapter Eleven

Problem # 10

There are no positive consequences
for good performance.

"Outstanding leaders go out of their way to boost
the self-esteem of their personnel. If people believe in themselves,
it's amazing what they can accomplish."

Sam Walton

J erry McGuire was a hit movie in 1996. Even today you still hear people using its most famous line: "SHOW ME THE MONEY!!!" Many leaders mistakenly believe that the only way to reward people is by showing them the money. Often, they feel frustrated because their company's compensation policies limit their ability to use money as a reward.

Money, however, is but one form of reward. *If you can't control financial rewards to the extent you like, focus on what you can control.* Tune into radio station WII FM or "What's In It For Me?" Most of your people do. Recognizing and rewarding good performance is the best way to ensure that people will continue to perform well.

The applause of a single human being is of great consequence.

Samuel Johnson

Almost everyone likes a pat on the back or a kind word now and then. You can use this to your advantage by recognizing and rewarding people who do what they are supposed to do. You have two opportunities to do this:

1) *People who are consistently good performers.* Most of the people you lead probably fall into this category. Recognize them for their consistency — for doing the right thing and getting things done the right way.

2) *People who have gone to extraordinary lengths.* If you look around, you'll probably see people doing heroic things everyday. These people need your recognition too — or they might not continue going to such extraordinary lengths.

You have to recognize outstanding efforts and/or consistently good performance if you want it to continue. Most people do not want or need constant reinforcement, but almost everyone needs and appreciates an occasional sincere "thank you" for their efforts.

My father gave me the greatest gift anyone could give

another person, he believed in me.

Jim Valvano

Specific, sincere feedback is the best way to provide some positive consequences for good performance. Don't just tell someone that she "has done a good job." Instead, pinpoint what the person did, how it relates to her goals and/or responsibilities, and why it is important to the specific work group and to the company in general.

Make sure that your feedback is timely. Positive reinforcement that follows soon after a particular action is much more effective than feedback given later in a performance review. Do it while the action or situation is fresh in both your minds. Here are some pointers on how to do this.

Get yourself ready for a recognition conversation by determining exactly why you want to recognize this person. Usually it's because he or she is meeting the expectations that have been set; has done an outstanding job on a particular project; or is a consistently good performer.

Good leaders make people feel that they're at the very heart of things, not at the periphery. They help everyone feel that he or she makes a difference to the success of the organization. When this happens people feel centered, and that gives their work meaning.

Warren Bennis

Begin the conversation by telling the individual that you want to compliment them on their performance. Be specific about what he or she did, and why this level of performance is important. This is an important step. Make sure you explicitly connect the person's performance with the big picture. Don't neglect it.

Explain that this type of performance not only results in company success, but sets an example for the entire work team.

Listen to what the person says. It's a sad commentary on modern organizational life, but many people are uncomfortable with compliments from their leader. Don't let him or her minimize the accomplishment. Make sure he or she knows that you think this level of performance is important.

This type of discussion has the potential to elicit good ideas from the individual. He or she has already demonstrated competence in meeting expectations and standards. Therefore, he or she might have some good ideas. Ask for any suggestions for improving departmental effectiveness.

Be careful here. You don't want to push. You want to make sure that the individual understands you are asking because he or she is a good performer, and not that you are just looking for ways to get more work out of them. The person should feel flattered that you are asking for his or her opinion, not as if you are punishing them for good performance — avoid the bony fingers syndrome.

Listen to what the individual says. As always, listen not just for content, but for the feelings and emotions behind the content. Go out of your way to use any of the suggestions that you can. If there is only a glimmer of a good idea there, build on it. Allow the employee to own the idea. Explain how you will use the ideas the two of you have come up with. Enlist his or her help in implementing them. If you can't use a suggestion, explain why.

End the discussion by coming back to the beginning. Thank the person again for his or her performance. Indicate your intention to act on the suggestions the two of you have agreed on.

The common sense leadership point here is: *People continue to do the things for which they get rewarded, so reward them for doing the things you want them to do.*

You have it easily in your power to increase the sum total of this world's happiness now. How? By giving a few words of sincere appreciation to someone who is lonely or discouraged. Perhaps you will forget tomorrow the kind words you say today, but the recipient may cherish them over a lifetime.

Dale Carnegie

Chapter Twelve

Problem #11

There are no negative consequences
for poor performance.

"When the eagles are silent, the parrots begin to jabber."
Winston Churchill

No matter how well you run your operation, and how good a job you do as a leader, you are still likely to run into some people with poor performance. Just as people should experience positive consequences for good performance, they should experience negative consequences for poor performance. Effective leaders have the will to address and fix poor performance — even when it's unpleasant to do so.

If you've been paying attention, you've probably tried a number of things to turn around poor performance. You've:

1. *Told people exactly what you expect of them.*

2. Explained the reasons why what you expect of them is important.

3. Taught them how to do what they need to do.

4. Explained why they need to do things in the right way.

5. Taught them the "genius of the and."

6. Made sure that they knew they were not performing in an acceptable manner when they started to slip.

7. Stopped rewarding non-performance.

8. Made sure that good performance is not punishing.

9. Removed obstacles to good performance.

10. Provided rewards and recognition for good performance.

People need to be reminded more often than

they need to be instructed.

Samuel Johnson

If all these things have failed, negative consequences are your next step. Negative consequences can range from things like increased interaction and scrutiny on your part, to the withholding of positive consequences like raises and promotion, to formal disciplinary action up to, and including, termination.

Negative consequences need not be heavy-handed. With most people, all you have to do is give them a gentle reminder — a tap on the shoulder, or a brief discussion, to get them back on track.

Leaders who judiciously administer negative consequences send a signal to the entire organization that they will not countenance poor performance over the long run. Delivering negative consequences is never fun or easy. However, if you're going to lead, somewhere along the line you'll have to do so. A few things to remember:

1. *Most people will perform well as long as they know what to do and how to do it.*

2. *The great majority of people will need little more than a gentle nudge (a conversation about how they are failing to meet expectations) to get them back on track.*

3. *When a nudge doesn't work, a kick in the butt (an explicit statement of the potential negative consequences) usually does the trick.*

4. *When a kick in the butt doesn't work, a 2X4 to the head (the experience of negative consequences) might be necessary.*

Needless to say, nudges are better than kicks in the butt and 2X4s to the head. Don't develop a punitive attitude. Negative consequences should be used as a last resort. However, people who won't or can't bring their performance up to standard need to feel some pressure to turn around their behavior and results.

The ultimate leader is one who is willing to develop

people to the point that they eventually surpass him

or her in knowledge and ability.

Fred A. Manske, Jr.

Here's an example that came up a few months ago with one of my clients. This particular client had a supervisor who consistently produced good numbers. However, he accomplished this through micro-management, fear and intimidation. People produced well for him, but they left his department as soon as they could find a way out. The supervisor in question operated from a "tyranny of the or" perspective. He would say things like: "What do you want? I can be a nice guy and everyone will like me, or I can make sure people do what they're supposed to do. I choose the latter. In that way, I can be sure that we'll make our numbers."

His boss tried having a "genius of the and" conversation with him, but his behavior didn't change. In fact, it seemed to get worse as he suspected that his people were complaining about him behind his back.

The manager resolved the situation by not giving the supervisor a promotion that he thought he deserved, and most everyone else thought he was sure to get. When he asked why, the manager told him that while achieving results is important, how the results are achieved is equally important, and that he didn't measure up in the latter category.

This negative consequence (the withholding of a promotion) was what it took to get this supervisor to turn around his behavior. The benefits were twofold. The supervisor finally got the message and changed his behavior. However, and maybe more important, the manager let everyone else know, in a subtle way, that he had heard their complaints about the supervisor and that he acted on them — by promoting someone else.

Take your obligation to redirect the behavior of people who are failing to meet results seriously. How well you do in redirecting people who are not meeting expectations can make or break you as a leader. When one of your people falls short of meeting expectations, take action quickly. Here are some pointers on how to go about administering negative consequences of poor performance.

Meet with the individual to review the expectations and his or her lack of performance in meeting them. Be specific about the expectations on which both of you have agreed, and the individual's lack of performance as measured by the standards. Once you've agreed on the specifics, work with the individual to develop a plan for bringing the performance up to expectations. This type of discussion is not punishment. It is intended to accomplish two things: 1) to alert the individual that his or her performance is not meeting expectations; and 2) to assist the individual in developing a plan for getting his or her performance back on track. This type of conversation is a "nudge."

Approach nudge discussions with goodwill in your heart. Your main concern should be to help the individual perform at an acceptable level. In most cases, it is appropriate to conduct two or three nudge discussions prior to moving on and administering more severe negative consequences.

Occasionally a nudge will not have the desired outcome. The individual in question will not bring his or her performance up to a level that meets the agreed on expectations. If this happens you need to ratchet it up a bit to a "kick in the butt" conversation.

A kick in the butt conversation should go something like this. Meet with the individual. Review the expectations and the individual's performance when measured against them. Review the action plan he or she developed in the previous conversation. Probe to determine why he or she has not been able to get their performance up to standard. Settle on another plan of action to help the person bring his or her performance up to standard.

Then, get to the kick in the butt part of the conversation. Inform the individual of the potential consequences (written warning, suspension, etc.) of continued lack of improvement. Don't threaten, but be very clear on what will happen if he or she does not bring his or her performance up to standard.

A kick in the butt discussion is intended to accomplish three things: 1) to alert the individual that his or her performance is still not meeting expectations; 2) to assist the individual in developing a plan for getting his or her performance back on track; and 3) to alert the individual to the positive consequences associated with improved performance or the negative consequences associated with continued lack of improvement.

Do not enter into this type of conversation lightly. You must be ready to deliver the promised consequences if the employee does not bring his or her performance up to standard in a reasonable amount of time. I suggest discussing the matter with your manager and a Human Resources professional prior to conducting this type of discussion. In this way, you'll be sure that you are acting in a manner consistent with the established practice of your company and work unit.

In most cases, a nudge or a kick in the butt discussion will fix your performance problem. However, in the rare event that they don't, you'll need to conduct a "2X4 to the head" conversation.

Before doing so, it is a good idea to discuss the situation with your manager and a Human Resources professional.

Never look down on a man unless you are helping him up.

Jesse Jackson

A 2X4 discussion is similar to a kick in the butt discussion, only this time you'll be administering the negative consequence, not just describing it. Even though you'll be delivering a negative consequence, you should approach this type of conversation with the goal of assisting the individual in raising his or her performance to a level where he or she meets the expectations of their position.

The common sense leadership points here are: *Deliver negative consequences when you must. Take it slowly step by step. Don't use a kick in the butt or a 2X4 to the head when a gentle nudge will do.*

Chapter Thirteen

〜

Performance Problems: Conversation Basics

"It was impossible to get a conversation going,

everybody was talking too much."

Yogi Berra

Your ability as a leader to engage in meaningful conversations with the people you lead is critical to solving performance problems. Conducting effective leadership conversations — especially about performance problems — can seem like a daunting task. However, it's not all that hard. I have developed a common sense, six-step model for conducting leadership conversations.

1. *Preparation*
2. *Opening*
3. *Information Sharing*
4. *Decision*
5. *Closing*
6. *Post Conversation Analysis*

No matter what type of leadership conversation you are conducting, you'll need to cover each of these six components. If you learn and master the skills and techniques associated with the steps in the model, you'll be able to conduct the most difficult leadership conversations and fix any performance problem that comes your way.

Step 1 — Preparation

One of my early mentors had a saying: "preparation makes up for a lack of talent." Preparation is the key to successful performance problem conversations. While it's critically important, it doesn't have to take a lot of your time. There are a few key things to remember about preparation.

First, determine your objective for the conversation. What outcome do you expect?

Second, gather and review all of the information you'll need in the conversation. If you're trying to fix a performance problem, you'll need to prepare by gathering information about the individual's performance in the problem area. What are the standards associated with the task? How is the person doing? What behavior do you want to reinforce? Why? What behavior do you want to redirect? Why? What does the individual do that hampers his or her effectiveness? What examples of specific behaviors will you cite to make and reinforce your points?

Third, think about the person with whom you'll be having the conversation. What is his or her likely reaction to your message? How will he or she feel about what he or she is hearing? Will he or she be sad, angry, frustrated? Once you have determined the other person's likely reaction to what you are saying, you'll need to plan your response. This is an old sales trick. Ever notice how a good salesperson seems to have an answer for every reason you raise for not wanting to buy his or her product or service? This isn't by accident. It's because he or she anticipated all of the potential objections that might come up. Then, he or she prepared answers to counter each of these objections. The same is true for effective leaders. They anticipate the possible reactions to the points they'll be making in their discussions with the people they lead. Then, they plan their response. In this way, they are not likely to get knocked off balance during the conversation.

If you take a few minutes to prepare for your leadership conversations by determining an objective for every conversation, identifying and reviewing all the information you'll be covering, and anticipating the other person's reactions to what you will say, your conversations will go smoothly. You'll be more confident, as you'll feel in command of your facts and the discussion. This confidence will be apparent to the other person. He or she will be more likely to respond well to you and your leadership.

Step 2 — Opening

A successful opening is the key to any leadership conversation. In the opening, you are laying the groundwork for the conversation. You need to let the other person know why you are having this conversation, why you think it is important and what you hope to get out of the conversation. A good opening does more than just set the stage. It puts the other person at ease, and gets him or her into a receptive frame of mind. Leadership conversations go much smoother when both parties are on the same page.

Step 3 — Information Sharing

Once you've opened the conversation and set the stage, it's time to get all of the information pertaining to the subject at hand out on the table. It's best to start by listening. Ask the other person for his or her thoughts on the topic. Listen attentively. Ask questions to clarify any points that are unclear. Paraphrase what he or she says to demonstrate your understanding.

Add your thoughts on the topic only after the other person has

exhausted his or hers. It's really important to let the other person
go first. If you begin by expressing your views, you run the risk of
having the other person clam up, or merely parrot back what you
have already said. You want to avoid this, as it can lead to a one-way
discussion. Your goal is to have a two-way, mutual, free flowing
discussion of the topic at this point. You're trying to open up
communication, not close it down.

Once you are reasonably sure that the two of you have
exhausted the issues surrounding the topic, review and summarize
the information before moving on to the next phase of the
conversation.

Step 4 — Decision

Begin this phase of the conversation the same way as the
previous one. Ask the other person for his or her ideas on how
you should proceed. Listen, ask questions and paraphrase, just as
you did in the *Information Sharing* phase. Look for suggestions that
you can adopt. Failing that, look for the glimmer of an idea in
something the other person has said. Build on this. In this way, he
or she will see that you are trying to use his or her ideas.

Add ideas of your own, but always credit the other person if
her or she has contributed to them in even the smallest way. If the
other person is a seasoned high performer, let him or her take the
lead in choosing the course of action. If he or she is new to the job

or a poor to mediocre performer, you'll have to take the lead.

Once you are in agreement on how you'll proceed, determine who is going to do what. Be clear on what you'll do, and what you are expecting of the other person. Set timelines so you can measure your progress.

Step 5 — Closing

Just as effective leadership conversations begin on a positive note, they need to end that way too. You want to do three things as you close a conversation: 1) summarize the discussion and the agreements you reached; 2) set a follow up date to review progress – a definite follow up date indicates that you're serious about what you've just discussed and the agreements you reached, and it motivates the other person to actually do something; and 3) express your confidence in the individual's ability to handle the situation you've just discussed.

Step 6 — Post Conversation Analysis

Effective leadership conversations are not isolated events. Therefore, you need to do a post conversation analysis of all of your conversations. Effective post conversation analyses focus on three things: 1) The result of the conversation: did you accomplish your objective? 2) Next steps: when will you have your next conversation with this employee? What will you want to discuss?

What do you want to pay attention to in the interim? 3) Your performance in the conversation: how well did you follow the four step conversation model? What did you do especially well? Why? What will you do differently in subsequent conversations?

Take notes as you reflect. You should maintain a file for every one of your direct reports. Keep your notes in these files. Your notes will be invaluable when you begin to prepare for future conversations. They will help you determine your objective for these conversations.

In summary

I can't stress enough the importance of steps one and six. You'll be able to conduct effective leadership conversations on a consistent basis only after you've committed yourself to taking the time necessary to prepare for your conversations in advance, and to analyze their results. Preparation and analysis enhance your ability to conduct meaningful, effective leadership conversations. Don't skip these important steps.

Effective leadership conversations follow a process. Learn and use the process, and you'll be able to handle most any leadership conversation that comes your way.

Chapter Fourteen

*Conversational
Tools for Fixing
Performance Problems*

*"In organizations, real power and energy is generated through
relationships. The patterns of relationships and the capacities to form
them are more important than tasks, functions, roles, and positions."*
Margaret Wheatly

When it's all said and done, fixing performance problems is
about relationships. You build strong relationships with
the people you lead by engaging in three types of meaningful
conversations with them: 1) Expectation Setting; 2) Reinforcing
Effective Performance; and 3) Redirecting Ineffective Performance.

1) Expectation Setting

Expectation setting is the most basic job you have. Everything proceeds from a well-articulated and communicated set of expectations. You have to make sure that your people know exactly what you expect of them. If your people don't know what you expect of them, you can't hold them responsible for the outcome of their work.

Just as archers have a target with concentric rings that forms a bulls eye, and bowlers have ten pins set up at the end of the alley, people at work need to have a clear, unambiguous target for which to aim. Be specific about what you expect from the people you lead.

Life is lived as a series of conversations.

Mike Magee

Meet face-to-face with your people to discuss and agree on expectations. Once a year, at the beginning of the year, is usually enough. However, in today's fast-paced world, things have a way of changing. When things change, clarify any changes in your expectations of your people. Everything flows from expectation-setting discussions. They are the foundation of successful leadership.

2) Reinforcing Effective Performance

People continue to do the things for which they get rewarded. Recognizing and rewarding people who perform well is an extremely important part of leadership. Unfortunately, many leaders do a poor job of giving rewards and recognition.

All too often leaders say: "I don't need to tell them when they're doing a good job. If they're not performing, they know they'll hear it from me." This is "high school principal leadership." As most of us remember, a summons to the principal's office was hardly ever good news. The same holds true in business. If the only interactions people have with you are negative or come with some type of punishment attached, they are not going to look forward to interacting with you. On the other hand, if you regularly recognize and reward people for good performance, you'll build strong, trusting, mutually accountable relationships with them.

Specificity and timeliness are the two keys to effective rewards and recognition. In most cases, merely telling someone that they "did a good job" is not effective. Such a statement lacks the specificity to make the compliment meaningful to the individual who receives it. On the other hand, telling someone that "they met or exceeded their production quota every day last week" passes the specificity test. The person being complimented knows exactly why he or she is being recognized.

Timeliness is the second key. The best recognition comes soon after the event that precipitated it. Effective leaders speak with their people regularly. They take the time to let people know when they're doing a good job.

3) Redirecting Ineffective Performance

If you do nothing more than set expectations and recognize your people when they do a good job, you're well on the road to success. However, you earn your money when you have to redirect ineffective performance. You're in business to help your people succeed. Many, if not most, will succeed if you do a good job of setting expectations. However, some will require additional coaching to be successful.

Take your obligation to redirect the behavior of people who are failing to meet expectations seriously. How well you do in redirecting people who are not meeting expectations can make or break you as a leader.

When one of your people falls short of meeting expectations, take action quickly. Meet with him or her to review the expectations and his or her lack of performance in meeting them. Be specific about the expectations on which both of you have agreed, and the individual's lack of performance as measured by the standards. Once you've agreed on the specifics, work with the individual to develop a plan for bringing the performance up to a satisfactory level.

Don't view this type of conversation as punishment. You want to accomplish two things: 1) alert the individual that his or her performance is not meeting expectations; and 2) assist him or her in getting back on track. Always approach these types of discussions with goodwill in your heart. Your main concern should be to assist the people you lead in performing at an acceptable level.

He that gives good advice, builds with one hand; he that

gives good counsel and example, builds with both.

Francis Bacon

In the end leading is as simple as 1, 2, 3. If you want to be an effective leader, become skilled in three types of discussions: 1) Expectation Setting; 2) Coaching; and 3) Performance Review.

Chapter Fifteen

One Last Thing... Dealing With Anger

*"If you are patient in one moment of anger,
you will escape a hundred days of sorrow."*
Chinese Proverb

I f you deal with poor performance, you will encounter anger inevitably. Anger is a funny thing. It can erupt at times when you least expect it. Many leaders are afraid of anger — their own and that of those they lead. However, if you have the courage to confront anger, you'll find that you'll be able to work through it, and that you'll gain the respect and admiration of the people you lead. Dealing with anger is just another part of being in the arena.

Dealing with anger is not fun or pleasant, but it is part of every leader's job. The best way to deal with anger is to be prepared for it. That way, you'll be able to handle it when and where it shows up. Here are five tips for dealing with anger:

1. *Acknowledge the anger.*
2. *Stay calm.*
3. *Ask questions.*
4. *Move from anger to solutions.*
5. *Develop a plan – and stick to it.*

1. Acknowledge the anger. People hate it when they are angry and feel as if they are being ignored. The best thing to do is make sure the other person knows that you are serious about the situation. Listen. Take notes. Be patient. Don't interrupt. Show empathy.

2. Stay calm. It will do you no good to get into a fight. Leaders who respond in kind to anger often come to regret it. Don't let another individual goad you into saying something that you don't want to say.

3. Ask questions. You can calm down an angry person by asking questions. After you let the person vent for a reasonable time, get specific. Try to find out exactly why the other person is angry. Find out what he or she wants you to do to correct the problem.

4. Move from anger to solutions. This is where you earn your money as a leader. After you get the person to calm down, get constructive.

Focus on helping the individual understand that he or she needs to improve his or her performance and that you are there to help — not just to criticize. Help the other person come up with constructive ideas for improving his or her performance. If they are having a difficult time coming up with ideas, propose something specific. Look for a quick hit — something that will show some immediate results. Don't argue over minor points — get some ideas on the table and agree on what he or she is going to do.

Speak when you are angry — and you will make the best

speech you'll ever regret.

Laurence J. Peter

---

5. *Develop a plan – and stick to it.* Once you've agreed on actions and a solution, set up a schedule to make sure the solution gets done. Set a realistic time frame. Follow up with the other person to make sure that he or she is meeting the milestones on which you've agreed.

While dealing with anger is never fun or pleasant, this simple five-step process will help you successfully turn anger into opportunity for improved performance. The common sense point here is: *Be prepared for anger, so you'll know exactly what to do when it comes up.*

Chapter Sixteen

Putting It All Together

"Leadership is not so much about technique and methods as it is about opening the heart. Leadership is about inspiration — of oneself and of others. Great leadership is about human experiences, not processes. Leadership is not a formula or a program, it is a human activity that comes from the heart and considers the hearts of others. It is an attitude, not a routine. Today, many followers believe they are part of a system, that lacks heart. If there is one thing a leader can do to connect with followers at a human level, it is to become engaged with them fully, to share experiences and emotions, and set aside the processes of leadership learned by rote."

Lance Secretan

By now you should have a pretty good idea of the reasons for poor performance — and what to do about each of them. Just to be on the safe side, the following pages review each problem, and how to fix it.

Problem:

People don't know what they are supposed to do.

Why This Happens:

- Leaders don't set clear expectations and standards
- Leaders don't communicate clear expectations and standards
- Leaders don't reinforce clear expectations and standards

How To Fix It:

- Use the **SMART** technique to clarify your expectations.

  - **S**pecific: Expectations should be targeted, not broad and general. They should be unambiguous and explicit. They should be clearly understood by any number of different people.

  - **M**easurable: You should be able to tell quickly and easily if an individual has met a standard or expectation. You should develop a set of criteria that will be indicative of success or failure in meeting expectations or standards.

  - **A**chievable: You'll want to set expectations and standards that are challenging, but not incredibly difficult to achieve. A challenging expectation is motivating, an impossible one is demotivating.

  - **R**esults Oriented: Avoid the activity trap. Your expectations should focus on the results you expect people to achieve, not the activities they will undertake to get there. For example, "improved presentation skills" is a result; "participating in a presentation skills training program" is an activity.

  - **T**ime Specified: People need to know the deadlines associated with expectations and standards. In a manufacturing environment, time frames may be very short (i.e. X number of pieces per shift). In a sales environment, time frames may be longer (i.e. $X sales per month).

- You should develop clear expectations and standards for every position that reports to you. Make sure you understand in your own mind the output you expect from that position regardless of the individual who fills it.

- Once you have a clear picture of your expectations of the positions reporting to you, communicate them to the individual(s) who occupy these positions. Explain three things:
  - What needs to be accomplished.
  - The deadline for accomplishing it.
  - What successful completion of the goal or task looks like.

- The more you keep your expectations in the forefront of people's minds, the more likely they will be to focus their attention and efforts on achieving them. Never miss an opportunity to reinforce them with the people you lead.

No one lives long enough to learn everything

they need to learn starting from scratch.

To be successful, we absolutely, positively have to

find people who have already paid the price to learn the

things that we need to learn to achieve our goals.

Brian Tracy

Problem:

*People don't know why they should do
what they are supposed to do.*

Why This Happens:

- People don't understand the business reasons for the expectations and standards.

- People don't understand the personal benefits that will accrue to them by meeting the expectations and standards.

How To Fix It:

- Make sure there is a good business reason for your expectations.

- If you can't find good business reasons, consider changing or modifying your expectations.

- Explain the business reason for your expectation, i.e.
    - "We are ISO certified. This means that we have developed and documented a set of procedures. We have to follow our procedures or we could lose our ISO certification. ISO certification is a condition of doing business with several of our biggest customers. We need to maintain our certification in good standing."

- Tune into radio station WII FM (What's In It For Me?). Make sure you can explain how meeting your expectations will personally benefit the people you lead.

- Personal benefits often include but are not limited to:
    - Improved customer satisfaction, leading to increased sales;
    - Increased sales, leading to profitability, which leads to job security;
    - Better knowledge and mastery of the skills necessary to meet the expectation, making the job easier;
    - Easier indentification and solution problems by use of a documented, consistently applied process.

Problem:

People don't know how to do what they are supposed to do.

Why This Happens:

- Leaders make assumptions about the level of knowledge and skill their people possess.
- People have not received proper training.
- People have not had to use a specific skill in some time.
- Job requirements have changed.
- People have lapsed into bad habits, and forgotten what they know.

How To Fix It:

- Observe your people, determine if they have the proper skills and training to do what is expected of them.

- Identify new skills necessitated by a change in job requirements.

- When people don't have the necessary skills, job requirements have changed, or they have lapsed into bad habits, teach them the correct way to do things.

- Use the Tell, Show, Observe, Reinforce, Redirect teaching model:

    - Tell the person what to do.

    - Show the person what to do.

    - Observe the person as he or she performs the task.

    - Reinforce correct or effective performance.

    - Redirect incorrect or ineffective performance.

Problem:

People think your ideas won't work or that they have a better way.

Why This Happens:

- Today's employees think for themselves; they are likely to challenge instructions that don't make sense to them.

- Leaders don't deal with employee challenges and concerns in an open and respectful manner.

How To Fix It:

- Make sure people *understand* your expectations.
    - Understanding is about the head. If you want people do something in a prescribed manner, take the time to explain not only how to do it correctly, but why it is important to do it that way.
- Make sure people *accept* your expectations.
    - Acceptance is about the heart. Understanding is a good start. But it's not always enough. If people don't like the reasons you've provided them, you won't get very far by re-explaining your reasons and logic. Instead, engage the other person in conversation. Listen to their side of things, empathize with them. Often, the mere act of listening to and empathizing with an individual's concerns is enough to get the person to change his or her behavior. If this doesn't work, try another tack. Ask him or her to suggest an alternative method. If you do this, make sure you set clear boundaries. If the individual comes up with good suggestions use them. If they don't, that's okay. Just being invited to participate goes a long way to ensuring acceptance.
- Make sure people can *do* what is necessary to meet your expectations.

- Doing is about the hands. It also is the leadership intervention most often used inappropriately. If an individual does not understand or accept instructions, merely showing him or her how to do things the right way is not going to help. It's like speaking louder in English to a non-English speaking person. All it does is frustrate both parties. On the other hand, there are times when focusing on doing is the correct thing to do. For example, a sales manager may notice that a salesperson is doing a poor job of integrating sales aids into his or her sales presentations. This may be because he or she: a) doesn't get the importance and usefulness of sales aids (understand); b) doesn't like the sales aids provided, and would rather use his or her own (accept); or c) doesn't know how to use sales aids effectively (do). If the real reason is "c", he or she doesn't know how to use sales aids effectively, some remedial training is the way to go. If it is "a" or "b", training on how to use sales aids is not likely to be effective.

A competent leader can get efficient service

from poor troops, while on the contrary

an incapable leader can demoralize

the best of troops.

General John J. Pershing

Problem:

People think other tasks and activities are more important.

Why This Is Happens:

- Most jobs have multiple priorities. Often people focus on one to the exclusion of others.
- People are often victims of "the tyranny of the or."
  - "What do you want, production or quality? I can't do both."
  - "What's more important, making sales calls or filling out reports? I can't do both."

How To Fix It:

- Keep people focused on all of the key indicators of their jobs.
- Help them understand that their jobs have a number of priorities, and all are important.
- Don't accept the "tyranny of the or."
- Focus people on the "genius of the and."
    - "I want you to meet production targets *and* meet quality standards *and* do it safely *and* in a manner that complies with all the regulations that govern manufacturing."
    - "I want you to make sales calls *and* close deals *and* complete all of your sales reports on time."

Problem:

People think they are performing in an acceptable manner.

Why This Happens:

- Leaders do not provide any performance feedback.
- In the absence of feedback, people assume they are doing a good job.
  - Employment laws are written to protect people who receive no feedback.

How To Fix It:

- Don't make people guess.
- Provide everybody who works for you with ongoing, timely feedback.
  - The goal of feedback is to help employees succeed by reinforcing effective performance or redirecting ineffective performance.
  - Feedback should be based on specific, observable or verifiable data and information.
  - Feedback should be delivered as close to the occurrence as possible.
  - Feedback should be a two-way process: ask the other person for input on why his or her performance is good or lacking.
  - Feedback should include a discussion of the potential impact of continued good performance or lack of performance.
  - Feedback should never be a threat or a promise.
  - Effective feedback, even when discussing poor performance, is perceived as helpful by the person receiving it.

Problem:

Non-performance is rewarded.

Why This Happens:

- Leaders fix the problems that their people make.

- Leaders take away the difficult or unpleasant jobs that their people do poorly.

- Leaders promote or transfer problem people — to get them out of their work group.

- Leaders pay too much attention to problem performers.

How To Fix It:

- Make your people handle their own problems.
  - Sometimes it seems easier to fix a problem yourself than to have the person responsible fix it. Avoid "subordinate-imposed time." Subordinate-imposed time begins the moment you take responsibility for something for which one of your people is responsible. It doesn't end until you return the responsibility to the proper person. Don't clean up your people's messes. Make them do it. Guide them, give them suggestions and help, but make them solve their own problems.
- Make everyone carry his or her own weight.
  - When people continually screw up a certain job or jobs, many leaders give up, and take away those jobs. They give them to someone they can trust. Pretty soon, the one or two people who they can trust are doing all the work, while everyone else is coasting. Insist that all of your people do a good job on the jobs for which they are responsible. Coach, advise and teach; but hold people accountable and responsible for doing their jobs. Keep the workload fair and evenly balanced.
- Never reward poor performers with promotions and transfers.
  - Do your best to turn around poor performance. Failing

this, work on an exit strategy. Don't pass your problems on to someone else by promoting or transferring poor performers. Fix the problem, don't pass it around like a box of Cracker Jack.

- Don't give undue attention to your problem performers.
  - The last problem is easy to slip into. However, spending a disproportionate amount of time with problem performers creates two potential problems:
    1) Problem performers get more attention than they deserve. Often problem performers are starved for attention. They prefer negative attention to no attention at all. They are like children who throw tantrums when they feel their parents aren't paying enough attention to them. It's easy to fall into the trap of meeting people's attention needs by spending too much time with problem performers. Don't give problem performers undue attention. Let them know that you are not happy with their performance, give them some ideas on how to fix their problem, but make them fix it themselves.
    2) Good performers do not get recognition for their performance. If you avoid spending too much time with problem performers, you'll free up time to reward good performers. Recognizing good

performance is a much better use of your time than constantly looking over the shoulder of your poor performers.

Problem:

Good performance feels like punishment.

Why This Happens:

- Leaders reward good performance with more work and difficult or unpleasant tasks.
- Leaders don't reward high performers: they use the excuse "it's the system."
- Leaders take high performers for granted.
- Leaders don't listen to their high performers.

How To Fix It:

- Keep things balanced. Don't fall into the trap of having one or two "go to" people who get all of the difficult and time-sensitive assignments. Spread out the work evenly.

- If people are exceptional performers, find a way to reward them. If you can't get them a raise or bonus because of your compensation system, find some non-monetary way to reward them for their efforts.

- Make sure high performers know how much you value their performance. Give them plenty of encouragement and pats on the back.

- Pay attention to what your high performers have to say. Solicit their advice on solving problems. Use their suggestions whenever you can.

Problem:

There are no positive consequences for good performance.

Why This Happens:

- Leaders feel uncomfortable paying compliments.

- Leaders assume people know when they're doing a good job.

- Leaders think that money is the only way to reward someone.

How To Fix It:

- Never forget that people continue to do the things for which they get recognized and rewarded.

- Recognize and reward people for doing the things you want them to do.

- Recognize and reward two types of people:

  - Consistently good performers. Most of the people you lead probably fall into this category. Recognize them for their consistency — for doing the right thing and getting things done the right way.

  - People who have gone to extraordinary lengths to solve a problem. If you look around, you'll probably see people doing heroic things everyday. These people need your recognition too — or they might not continue going to such extraordinary lengths.

- Remember, most people don't want or need constant reinforcement, but almost everyone needs and appreciates an occasional sincere "thank you" for their efforts.

  - Specific, sincere feedback is the best way to provide positive consequences for good performance. Don't just tell someone that she "has done a good job." Instead, pinpoint what the person did, how it relates to her goals and/or responsibilities, and why it is important to the work group in particular, and the company in general. Make sure that your feedback is timely. Positive reinforcement that follows soon after a particular action is much more effective than feedback given later in a performance review.

Not everything that is faced can be changed.

But nothing can be changed until it is faced.

James Baldwin

FIXING PERFORMANCE PROBLEMS

Problem:

There are no negative consequences for poor performance.

Why This Happens:

- Leaders feel uncomfortable providing negative consequences.

122

How To Fix It:

- Don't accept poor performance over an extended period of time. If you do, you will lose credibility as a leader. As Winston Churchill said, "When the eagles are silent, the parrots begin to jabber."

- Remember:
  - Most people will perform well as long as they know what to do, why they should do it, and how to do it.
  - The great majority of people will need little more than a gentle nudge (a conversation about how they are failing to meet expectations) to get them back on track.
  - When a nudge doesn't work, a kick in the butt (an explicit statement of the potential negative consequences) usually does the trick.
  - When a kick in the butt doesn't work, a 2X4 to the head (the experience of negative consequences) is necessary.

- Approach these types of discussions with goodwill in your heart. Your main concern should be to get the individual's performance up to an acceptable level — not to punish him or her.

- Work with your Human Resources professionals to ensure that the negative consequences you deliver are in line with your company's philosophy and policies.

Problem:

People experience obstacles beyond their control.

Why This Happens:

- There are organizational policies, procedures and practices that prevent people from performing at a high level.
- People don't realize that they have the wherewithal to remove or overcome an obstacle.
- People don't have the skills necessary to do what it takes to perform well.

How To Fix It:

- Review your policies, procedures and practices to ensure that they are not hampering people's ability to perform.

  - Identify and change those that make it difficult for people to perform well. Eliminate "stupid rules" and you eliminate obstacles to effective performance.

- Reward people for identifying and fixing problem practices. Don't make them go crazy just trying to get someone's attention.

- Make sure that your people have both the willingness and ability necessary to do what it takes to perform well. Set them up to succeed, not fail.

  - *Willingness* is about commitment and confidence: your good example will go a long way towards instilling these qualities in your people.

  - *Ability* is about skills: give your people coaching, formal classes, on the job training and specific, ongoing feedback to help them improve.

- Do whatever you can to make it easy for your people to do their jobs.

Chapter Seventeen

Conclusion

Fixing performance problems is one of the most significant jobs of a leader. If you're a leader, it's simple. You have the responsibility of getting the best out of the people you lead. You can't ignore performance problems. You have to do something about them. That's why you're here…that's what is expected of you. You're a leader. You're in the arena everyday.

In this book, I've provided you with a review of the eleven most common types of performance problems, the reasons why they happen, and some common sense ideas for fixing them. To really fix any performance problem, you first have to determine the reason for it, and then apply the correct tool for fixing it.

If you've read carefully, you should know how to solve performance problems. You should have the knowledge it takes to fix any performance problem you encounter.

But knowing what to do is not enough. You have to put this

knowledge to work. Here's a story about putting knowledge to work.

When I was a growing up in Pittsburgh, my dad would sometimes come home from work with a pencil in his pocket. He was a steelworker. The pencils were US Steel issued and said "Knowing's not Enough." For some reason, these pencils fascinated me. I just couldn't figure out what "Knowing's not Enough" meant. I thought it must be something important — afterall, it was on all of these pencils. But I just didn't quite get it.

As I've gotten older, and hopefully wiser, I think I've figured out that statement. To me, it means something like this: people usually know what to do, but they often don't do it. They don't do it because other priorities get in the way, or it's too hard, or too tedious, or for any number of reasons.

Knowing what to do is not the same as doing it. If you don't use your knowledge, you might as well not have it. Many of us make up a million excuses for not doing what we know is the right thing to do rather than just going ahead and doing it. Like Mark Twain said, "The man who won't read good books has no advantage over the man who can't read them."

This book contains my best advice on solving performance problems. I hope you think it's good advice. I don't know if you do or don't. But I do know one thing. The only way you'll benefit from the advice in this book is by using it. Because afterall, knowing really is not enough — it's action that counts!

About the Author

Bud Bilanich's pragmatic approach to business, life, and the business of life has earned him the title The Common Sense Guy, and made him one of the most sought after speakers, consultants and executive coaches in the USA!

Dr. Bilanich's work focuses on improving the performance of individuals, teams and entire organizations. Bud is Harvard educated, but has a no-nonsense, common sense approach to his work that stretches back to his roots in the steel country of Western Pennsylvania. His consulting and coaching clients report that he is full of practical, useful common sense advice that they can put to work immediately. Audiences leave his Common Sense Keynotes armed with fundamentally sound, common sense ideas and the motivation to put those ideas to work.

Bud has 30 years experience in the organization effectiveness field. He has worked with clients in the US, Canada, Latin America, Europe, Australia and Asia. His clients include Pfizer Inc, Johnson and Johnson, Abbott Laboratories, Schein Pharmaceuticals, General Motors, Citicorp, JP Morgan Chase, AT&T, Pitney Bowes, Dana Corporation and The Boys and Girls Clubs of America.

In addition to Fixing Performance Problems, he is the author of four books:

- *Four Secrets of High Performing Organizations*

- *Leading With Values*
- *Using Values To Turn Vision Into Reality*
- *Supervisory Leadership In The New Factory*

Bud is a prolific writer. You can find his thoughts on contemporary business topics and issues on his popular blog: www.CommonSenseGuy.com. You can find more information on his work at his website: www.BudBilanich.com.

Dr. Bilanich received an EdD from Harvard University with a concentration in Organizational Behavior and Intervention. He also holds an MA in Organizational and Interpersonal Communication from the University of Colorado, and a BS in Human Development from Penn State.

He is a member of several professional organizations: National Speakers Association, American Society for Training and Development, International Coach Federation, Association of Business Communicators, National Storytelling Association.

Bud is a cancer survivor. He lives in Denver, CO with Cathy, his wife. He is a retired rugby player, an avid cyclist, and a film, live theatre and crime fiction buff.